IMPACT
MAKING A DIFFERENCE
FOR ETERNITY

Jeannette Luby

IMPACT
MAKING A DIFFERENCE
FOR ETERNITY

CONTENTS

Acknowledgements

Thank You to my Savior, Lord, King, Messiah, Jesus Christ, for loving me, saving me, and forgiving me. He has changed my life forever. I will never be the same. Thank You for calling me Your own.

Secondly, I want to thank my dear husband, John, for his prayers, support, and patience as I completed another assignment from the Lord. He is my best friend, encourager, sweetheart, and biggest fan. You are the best, my love.

Thank you to my daughter, Candice Hampton, for her prayer support, creative and technical input, encouragement, and expertise in editing. You are my friend and cheer leader.

I am so grateful for the prayers, support, and encouragement of my pastors, Drs. James and Cathie Hightshoe, while on this adventure writing. Your help with editing, guidance, wise counsel, and friendship are wonderful, gracious gifts to me. Thank you for the investment of your time in this endeavor for the Kingdom. Thank you for being my pastors, being faithful to G-d, His Word, Holy Spirit's leading, and for your servant's hearts.

Thank you to Evangelists Mike and Sara Vidulich of MJV Ministries in Delray Beach, Florida. Thank you for your passion for G-d and for the lost. Thank you both for inspiring me to continue to be a soul winner every day, wherever I go. Thank you for your prayers, support, encouragement, and precious friendship.

Thank you to Pat and Steve Dahle, my dearest of friends and mentors. Thank you for your obedience to the Lord. Thank you for calling me up and out of where I was years ago and into the Destiny G-d has for me. I am grateful for your encouragement, your friendship, and the impartation and blessings you both have given me through your prophetic and apostolic anointing. The words the LORD spoke through you gave me life and hope.

And finally, thank you to my church family and friends. You all are a blessing to me and to the body of Christ as a whole. Each one of you is unique, called, and appointed a glorious Destiny in the Kingdom of G-d. It is my privilege to know you all and be a part of your lives. I love you and pray G-d's abundant blessings and favor on you and your families.

I pray you will go deeper and higher into the glory realm and your relationship with the Lord. I pray that you will know Him more every day as He gives you greater revelation of His love for you.

IMPACT
MAKING A DIFFERENCE FOR ETERNITY
By Jeannette Luby

Introduction

WHEN THE LORD spoke the word *impact* into my spirit, I didn't immediately know what He meant.

However, He gave me further revelation and instructions to write this book.

Even as believers in Jesus Christ, we do not know the full extent of the power that is accessible to us. Nor do we fully know the impact we can have on those around us and on the world.

You may be one who thinks, "What can I possibly *do* that will make a difference?" "How can *I* change the world for Christ?"

This book will answer those questions and more as you delve into the deep mysteries of G-d's universal principles.

I pray this book will give you knowledge of the truth and encourage you to grasp firmly to what G-d has already given you: the power of the Kingdom of G-d that lives in you! I pray this book will inspire you to step out in faith in obedience to the Lord. I pray that you would be a conduit for His truth and love in a powerful way to all those around you and to the world.

You *can* make a difference for the Kingdom of G-d! You *can* have an impact on the world for Jesus Christ!

What is Impact?

According to Merriam-Webster, the word *impact* means "to have a direct effect or impact on". Some synonyms listed are effect, touch, influence, reach, and move. Oxford Languages Dictionary defines *impact* as "to have a strong effect on someone or something". Included as synonyms with that definition are affect, influence, change, alter, modify, and transform.

The Dichotomy—
Catastrophe vs. Transformation

Our entire family loves science. We all enjoy different branches of science. My husband and I like astronomy as do our youngest grandsons. They are captivated by the stars, planets, meteorites, comets, nebulae, and anything to do with space outside the Earth's atmosphere.

What an amazing G-d we have. The Creator made everything perfectly. There is a beautiful, complete, and perfect balance in creation. It is fascinating how objects, thousands and even millions of miles away, can influence our everyday lives, such as our moon's orbit affecting the tides on Earth.

Over the years there have been "predictions" of asteroids and meteorites striking the Earth. The astronomers, who study the solar system and space, calculate the possibility of collisions with the Earth. The impact of an object contacting the Earth's surface would be catastrophic. It would change life on Earth as we know it, changing it forever.

We can see the effect of past meteorite impacts around the globe. These past cataclysmic events left huge craters, permanently marking their contact with the earth's surface.

In this regard, when something physical occurs, it results in a colossal disastrous event.

Physics is the branch of science that studies matter and energy, their interactions, and physical properties and processes. In physics, *impact* refers to physical contact. It has the implication of a violent disruption or an upheaval. It is a concussion which often suggests the shattering, disrupting, or weakening effects of a collision, explosion, or blow, such as a blast.

A *disruption* is "a break or interruption in the normal course or continuation of some activity, process, etc." It is an upheaval or disturbance. It can be positive or negative.

Oftentimes, we think of a physical impact as having a negative outcome. However, not every impact in the physical realm has a negative result. Not every disruption or upheaval is bad.

For instance, nuclear scientists and physicists have learned how to harness nuclear energy, through splitting uranium atoms (fission). It is a controlled chain reaction of the atomic particles colliding and splitting the atomic nuclei. When that happens, heat and radiation are released. The convective heat is used to produce steam, which is used by a turbine generator to generate electricity.

You might be wondering what astronomy and physics have to do with making a difference on the Earth for the Kingdom of G-d!

Just as when a physical impact happens in the physical realm, we can see a similar occurrence when we make a positive impact in the spiritual realm for the Kingdom of G-d. It results in a gloriously wonderful upheaval in a soul. A soul that was bound for eternal destruction in hell becomes one bound for eternal life in Heaven.

We make an *impact* in someone's life by sharing that G-d loves them, has a wonderful plan for their life, and they can know for sure that they are going to Heaven. Then, the "life course" they were on is disrupted. When they receive Jesus as their Savior and Lord, He alters, changes, and transforms their life forever. As they collide with the truth of His great and wondrous love for them, they will never be the same.

It is an impact that causes a divine transformation.

It is a Holy Ghost interruption, the best kind of interruption. For, it is one that will affect their life on Earth as well as their eternal life. It is one that will change their life forever.

BUT HOW WILL
THEY KNOW?

F OR THAT INTERRUPTION to happen, that life-changing collision with truth, someone must tell them. They need the information before they can, by their will receive it.

> "In fact, it says,
> 'The message is very close at hand; it is on your lips and in your heart.'
> And that message is the very message about faith that we preach: If you openly declare that Jesus is Lord and believe in your heart that G-d raised Him from the dead, you will be saved. For it is by believing in your heart that you are made right with G-d, and it is by openly declaring your faith that you are saved. As the Scriptures tell us, 'Anyone who trusts in Him will never be disgraced.' Jew and Gentile are the same in this respect. They

have the same Lord, who gives generously to all who call on Him. For 'Everyone who calls on the name of the Lord will be saved.'

But how can they call on Him to save them unless they believe in Him?

And how can they believe in Him if they have never heard about Him?

And how can they hear about Him unless someone tells them?

And how will anyone go and tell them without being sent? That is why the Scriptures say, 'How beautiful are the feet of messengers who bring good news!'"

Romans 10:8-15 NLT

Who will tell these lost souls? Will you?

You may think that it is a pastor's or an evangelist's job. It is our job. All believers are supposed to share the gospel. That is why we are here on the Earth.

It is true that not all of us are called to be pastors or missionaries. We may not be called to personally bring the gospel of Jesus Christ to China, Africa, or South America.

But we are all called to bring the gospel to the people in our "world", whatever our world looks like and whatever our world consists of. It could be a small rural town of 500 people, a workplace with 5,000 employees, or an office of two or three people. We are to bring the Good News to our family, friends, neighbors, town, city, county, region, and country.

Sometimes when we look at the big picture, we get overwhelmed. Even though we need to see the big picture, we need to focus on the part that G-d has for us to do *today*. How do we win an entire city for Christ?

I spoke with one of my pastors about this subject a few weeks ago. What Dr. Cathie Hightshoe said was so true, vital, and much needed. We can reach one person at a time with the gospel of Jesus Christ. We can make disciples for Jesus, one person at a time.

Dr. Hightshoe explained how each one of us can accomplish that by inviting people into our homes and telling them G-d loves them. We can open our lives, and ourselves to reaching the lost around us, one person at a time.

As we reach out to the people around us to meet their needs, whether feeding them, helping financially, or giving emotional and spiritual support, we need to tell them about Jesus. It is wonderful to show others kindness and help them and our communities but, if we don't tell them about G-d's love, kindness, and gift of salvation, our help to them is only temporary.

We need to share with them the One who is their provider, the One who loves, and wants a relationship with them. The point *is* for us to be the hands and feet of Jesus, *pointing them to Jesus!*

Most people come to salvation and faith in Jesus Christ because someone told them about Him. They shared their testimony and the gospel. Although some do come to salvation by randomly picking up a Bible and reading it, more people receive Christ because someone *told* them about Him.

Time and again, the Gospels tell about people who came to believe in Jesus. They believed because Jesus healed, delivered, and showed them His love. As a result, they went and told others what He did for them, sharing their good news. They shared their testimony.

Following are the lyrics of a popular song:

"If You're not in it
Then I don't want it
Let all else fade away
Take the whole world
Give me Jesus
Let all else fade away...

Here's my life, have Your way (Your way)
Your name is the only name that matters
And your heart is all that I desire
Not my will, but Yours alone forever
Here's my life, have Your way
Here's my life, have Your way
Here's my life, have Your way."

("Fade Away", written by Melodie Malone, Sean Curran & Jonathan Smith, Worship Together Music, 2019)

Just like the song says, we should want G-d in everything we do. He wants to and can be if we allow Him.

We should submit every area of our lives to Him. That includes submitting the part of our life where we hold back from sharing Him with others.

For us to make a difference in the world, we need to share the Good News with those in our world and then beyond!

For us to make an impact, a permanent mark, and a difference for eternity, we must share the gospel.

ONE AT A TIME

We don't have to share the gospel to a room full of people. We can share it over a cup of coffee with a neighbor, with the cashier at the grocery store, or with someone at the adjacent gas pump while filling up our tank. We can share with one person at a time.

G-d's Kingdom is a Kingdom of multiplication. G-d is a multiplier. When we sow a seed, G-d multiplies it. Whether it is our finances, time, or talents and giftings that are being sown into the Kingdom work, G-d multiplies what is sown. When we give to Him and sow into the Kingdom, He multiplies it. He does that with people, too.

That is how disciples are made. The Lord made disciples one person at a time.

Making disciples stems from our own faith, which we usually have because someone shared the gospel with us. Making disciples continues the cycle of G-d's redemptive power as we pass on our testimony to others. When we do that, it builds up the faith in the person with whom we are sharing. It also builds our faith.

This is how Kingdom multiplication works. We share the gospel with our neighbor. As a result, he receives Jesus as Savior and Lord in his life. Then, he tells someone he knows what G-d did for him and that person receives Jesus, too. The multiplicative cycle continues. That is the Kingdom of G-d.

WHY SHOULD I SHARE?

We need to share the gospel with others because G-d commands it. By doing so, we are obeying the Lord.

By faith, we are to obey. When we step out in faith and trust G-d, He empowers us to do what He commanded.

Each believer has faith, a gift from G-d. We need faith to believe and trust in Jesus as Savior and Lord. We need faith to believe that He is the Son of G-d and that He died for our sins, rose from the grave, lives in Heaven, and is coming back for us someday.

The way or means by which G-d brings salvation to us, is through faith. It is a gift from Him because of His great grace, mercy, and love for us.

Our part is to exercise the faith He has given us.

"You come to G-d by faith. Faith is G-d's currency. When you do things by faith, you please G-d. When the gift of faith is in operation, you tap into the supernatural realm." (Vidulich)

> *"For by grace you have been saved*
> *through faith, and that not of yourselves;*
> *it is the gift of G-d, not of works, lest*
> *anyone should boast."*

Ephesians 2:8-9 NKJV

We have been saved through faith in Jesus Christ and His shed blood as the payment for our sins. We are made righteous through faith in Him.

> *"But now the righteousness of G-d apart from*
> *the law is revealed, being witnessed by the*
> *Law and the Prophets, even the righteousness*
> *of G-d, through faith in Jesus Christ, to*
> *all and on all who believe. For there is no*
> *difference; for all have sinned and fall short*
> *of the glory of G-d, being justified freely*
> *by His grace through the redemption that*
> *is in Christ Jesus, whom G-d set forth as a*
> *propitiation by His blood through faith, to*
> *demonstrate His righteousness, because in His*
> *forbearance G-d had passed over the sins that*
> *were previously committed, to demonstrate at*
> *the present time His righteousness, that He*
> *might be just and the justifier of the one who*
> *has faith in Jesus."*

Romans 3:21-26 NKJV

From Where does
Faith Come?

W<small>E ALREADY DISCUSSED</small> that faith is a gift from
G-d, because of His grace and mercy. But how
does one get faith? How does one get faith to
believe in Jesus Christ and the gospel?

The Scriptures say that faith comes through hearing
the Word of G-d.

> *"So then faith comes by hearing, and hearing
> by the Word of G-d."*
>
> **Romans 10:17 NKJV**

The Apostle Paul wrote this in his letter to the
Christians in Rome.

Let's go back to see the context in which Paul wrote
this to give us a better understanding about *faith,* hearing
the Word, and salvation.

At the beginning of Romans chapter 10, Paul explains
to the church that his heart longs for the people of Israel
to believe in Jesus as Messiah, Savior, and Lord, so they
can be saved. He explains they are trusting in the old ways

of the law. Their faith was in obeying all G-d's command-ments to be right with G-d, rather than placing their faith in Yeshua (Jesus). They placed their faith in the law for their salvation.

Further, Paul says that nothing we do ourselves will save us and that, if we believe in our heart and declare or confess with our mouth that Jesus is Lord and G-d raised Him from the dead, we will be saved.

> *"That if you confess with your mouth the Lord Jesus and believe in your heart that G-d has raised Him from the dead, you will be saved. For with the heart one believes unto righteousness, and with the mouth confession is made unto salvation."*
>
> **Romans 10:9-10 NKJV**

And then Paul says,

> *"For "whoever calls on the name of the LORD shall be saved."*
>
> **Romans 10:13 NKJV**

He is quoting the Old Testament prophet, Joel.

> *"But everyone who calls on the name of the LORD will be saved,"*
>
> **Joel 2:32 NLT**

Faith, powerful enough to save, comes through hearing

the Word of G-d, the gospel of Jesus Christ, the Good News by the power of Holy Spirit!

That is why we need to share the gospel with others. They need to hear the Word of G-d, the Good News about G-d loving them and sending His only Son to die for their sins, so they can receive the gift of eternal life and be forgiven. Anytime the true, pure gospel of Jesus Christ is communicated in any way, whether spoken or read, there is the potential for *faith* to be birthed and come alive!

THE SUM X THE
EXPONENT = IMPACT

THERE IS AN equation so powerful that it can and will change the world. We need to bring the parts of the equation together. When we do, the product is beyond our imagination and comprehension! The impact is of the greatest magnitude!

The first addend in this divine equation is *faith*. The second addend is *obedience*. When we add obedience to our faith, the incredible result is beyond our finite thinking!

The apostle Luke wrote of an incident when Simon Peter fished all night and didn't catch anything. Jesus told him to take his boat out where the water was deeper and let the nets down.

Simon Peter said to the Lord,

> *"'Master,' Simon replied, 'we worked hard all last night and didn't catch a thing. But if you say so, I'll let the nets down again.' And this time their nets were so full of fish they began to tear! A shout for help brought their partners in the other boat, and soon both*

*boats were filled with fish and on the verge
of sinking. When Simon Peter realized what
had happened, he fell to his knees before Jesus
and said, 'Oh, Lord, please leave me—I'm
such a sinful man,' For he was awestruck by
the number of fish they had caught, as were
the others with him. His partners, James and
John, the sons of Zebedee, were also amazed.
Jesus replied to Simon, 'Don't be afraid! From
now on you'll be fishing for people!' And as
soon as they landed, they left everything and
followed Jesus."*

Luke 5:5-11 NLT

Simon Peter didn't feel like going out to try to catch fish again, since he had been doing that unsuccessfully all night. But, he did it anyway. He was obedient. He exercised his faith and trusted in Jesus to come through. G-d is always faithful. He always comes through with what He promises.

When we exercise our faith in obedience to G-d, G-d shows up and does miraculous things. That *is* tapping into the supernatural realm! (Vidulich)

We expect G-d to come through and do miracles, healing, signs, and wonders, but don't always exercise our faith in the little things He tells us to do, such as sharing the gospel with those around us.

You *can* do it, just as Simon Peter did.

Throw your net out, whatever that looks like; however

Holy Spirit leads you to do. Your net may be inviting neighbors over for dinner or paying for a babysitter so you can take a single mom out for coffee. It may be shoveling the driveway of an elderly person. It might be inviting the bank teller to church, volunteering at a food pantry, or driving someone to an appointment.

Will you toss your net into the deeper water?

Do it, and watch Jesus show up!

BEAUTIFUL FEET

A S PREVIOUSLY STATED, Scripture tells us faith comes by hearing the Word of G-d, the Good News of the Gospel.

> *"But how can they call on Him to save them unless they believe in Him? And how can they believe in Him if they have never heard about Him? And how can they hear about Him unless someone tells them? And how will anyone go and tell them without being sent? That is why the Scriptures say, 'How beautiful are the feet of messengers who bring good news!'"*
>
> **Romans 10:14-15 NLT**

Paul is quoting from the book of Isaiah in the above Scripture. Isaiah said the feet of those who bring good news are beautiful. In other words, the messengers of hope and life are wonderful and beautiful to those who are waiting to hear their message, words of light, love, life, and liberty. It is Good News for their souls, spirits, and bodies.

Messengers bring the Good News of salvation and hope of a future.

> *"How beautiful upon the mountains are the feet of him who brings good news,*
>
> *Who proclaims peace, who brings glad tidings of good things, who proclaims salvation, who says to Zion, 'Your G-d reigns!'"*
>
> **Isaiah 52:7 NKJV**

Jesus Himself gave us the directive to go into all the world and preach the gospel.

> *"Then the eleven disciples went away into Galilee, to the mountain which Jesus had appointed for them. When they saw Him, they worshipped Him; but some doubted. And Jesus came and spoke to them, saying, 'All authority has been given to Me in Heaven and on earth. Go therefore and make disciples of all the nations, baptizing them in the name of the Father and of the Son and of the Holy Spirit, teaching them to observe all things that I have commanded you; and lo, I am with you always, even to the end of the age.' Amen."*
>
> **Matthew 28:16-20 NKJV**

The world will hear and know when we go out of our way and out of our comfort zone to share the gospel with them. That is how they will hear and know the goodness of G-d, His redeeming love for them, and His forgiveness, freedom, and eternal life.

We are the ones who must make the impact. Impact takes an *action* in the physical *and* spiritual realm. We need to *act*, obeying G-d, so that the whole world will know Him.

Perhaps you have shared your testimony and the gospel with people, and they walked away, tried to convince you of their philosophies, or even became angry. Don't be discouraged! This happens to all of us, even those who are experienced soul-winners.

We are not responsible for how someone responds or reacts when we share the gospel with them. That is between them and G-d. Our responsibility is to tell them, to share it with them. Holy Spirit does the rest.

Be aware that the enemy does not want you to share Jesus with anyone. He wants to take everyone to hell with him.

Be encouraged and press on. There is a helpful resource at the end of this book to assist you in being an everyday soul-winner for Jesus.

G-d wants to use us to minister His love to people and share the gospel with them as we do so. We should be meeting their spiritual needs as we meet their physical needs and vice versa. But to do this, we must listen to the Lord for direction and then obey Him. We must look for opportunities all around us, wherever we go.

It is important that we hear G-d's voice, what He is

saying to us, and where He is sending us. And then, we need to obey Him.

Adding obedience to our faith is a powerful thing. Amazing and wonderful blessings come our way. We see signs, wonders, and miracles.

Our equation thus far—

(Faith + obedience)

We can see, know, and experience the fullness and completeness of the effectual power of the convergence of exercising one's faith and obeying the voice of the Lord. Doing so has an amazing and dynamic effect on one's own life, circumstances, and situations, as well as others' lives.

There is a third part to this spiritual equation which impacts our lives, others' lives, and the entire world for the Kingdom of G-d. It is *love*. When love, G-d's *agape* love, enters the equation, the effectual power exponentially increases beyond our human comprehension! It is His unconditional love that makes a difference.

Faith is *powerful*. Obedience is *powerful*. Add those two together in a gloriously divine equation and the sum of them is extraordinary! Raise that to the "agape love" power…and WOW! The *love* of G-d is *powerful*. The love of G-d is the most powerful thing one can ever experience! It is the passion of Christ, and the heart of the Father.

"But G-d is so rich in mercy, and He loved us so much, that even though we were dead because of our sins, He gave us life when He raised Christ from the dead. (It is only by G-d's grace that you have been saved!)"

Ephesians 2:4-5 NLT

"For this is how G-d loved the world: He gave His one and only Son, so that everyone who believes in Him will not perish but have eternal life. G-d sent His Son into the world not to judge the world, but to save the world through Him."

John 3:16-17 NLT

"The LORD has appeared of old to me, saying:
'Yes, I have loved you with an everlasting love;
Therefore with lovingkindness I have drawn you."

Jeremiah 31:3 NKJV

"But G-d demonstrates His own love toward us, in that while we were still sinners, Christ died for us."

Romans 5:8 NKJV

With the sum of faith and obedience multiplied by G-d's love, the product is a divine dynamic! The result is dynamic power! It *is* the *power* to change the world!

Following is the final equation:

$$(\textbf{\textit{Faith + obedience}})^{agape\ love}$$

Science and the Supernatural

S CIENCE IS THE pursuit of the application of knowledge and understanding of the natural and social world following a systematic methodology based on evidence. The supernatural are forces beyond scientific understanding or physical laws.

Science is limited to intellectual thought. It is limited to our mind and what we physically see and can comprehend. The supernatural is of the spiritual realm and, when it is from G-d, it is limitless in holy power to accomplish what G-d has in mind. It is beyond our comprehension and understanding. *That* is faith.

G-d's power is also supernatural, beyond scientific understanding or physical laws. Faith is supernatural.

> *"Faith shows the reality of what we hope for; it is the evidence of the things we cannot see. Through their faith, the people in days of old earned a good reputation. By faith we understand that the entire universe*

> *was formed at G-d's command, that what*
> *we now see did not come from anything*
> *that can be seen."*
>
> **Hebrews 11:1-3 NLT**

Therefore, in G-d's mighty, limitless power, we *can* have an impact and change the world for eternity. His power is like dynamite!

> *"But you will receive power when the*
> *Holy Spirit comes upon you. And you will*
> *be my witnesses, telling people about me*
> *everywhere—in Jerusalem, throughout Judea,*
> *in Samaria, and to the ends of the earth."*
>
> **Acts 1:8 NLT**

The word Luke used for power is *dynamis*. It transliterates to mean "force (literally or figuratively), especially miraculous power; a miracle itself." It also means "mighty deed, (worker of) miracle(s), power, strength, violence, mighty (wonderful) work."

The origins of the words *dynamite* and *dynamic* are from the Greek word *dynamis*.

We exercise our faith, and step out in it, we believe that G-d will be faithful to His Word. When we obey His mandate to share the gospel, not in our own strength, but with the compassion, power, and love of Jesus, then miraculous things happen!

The gospel is fresh, new, and vital every time we share

it! It is glorious and wonderful. It brings freedom and life. It brings forgiveness and hope.

Sharing Jesus should not be a chore. It should be a delight and blessing to those who are sharing and receiving. It should bring joy to all those involved.

Oftentimes, we worry that we don't know enough or won't remember the Scripture we memorized. The enemy wants us to be anxious, afraid, and to think we aren't going to do it right. Jesus came to set us free from sin and fear.

> *"For G-d has not given us a spirit of fear, but of power and of love and of a sound mind."*
> ### II Timothy 1:7 NKJV

When we step out in faith and obedience, the supernatural *dynamis* power of G-d becomes evident through the presence of His Holy Spirit in and through us.

OBJECTIONS
AND OBSTACLES

THE PURPOSE OF this book is to inspire and encourage you to do what G-d has called you to do.

There are different excuses people use for why they can't or won't go soul winning. I probably know most of them because I believed them myself.

One excuse I often used was *fear.*

I was afraid of rejection.

I was afraid I didn't know enough.

I was afraid I would sound stupid.

I was afraid I would offend someone.

I was afraid the person would get angry.

I was afraid the person would walk away.

I was afraid I would say the wrong thing.

I was afraid I wouldn't remember Scripture verses to share.

I was afraid the person would not want to receive Jesus as their Savior.

I was afraid I couldn't answer all the possible questions someone might ask.

I simply was *afraid*.

> *"Such love has no fear, because perfect love expels all fear."*
>
> **I John 4:18a NLT**

The second big obstacle I faced was that I didn't think I knew enough.

When we look in Scripture, the people that Jesus ministered to, the ones He physically healed and set free from demons, excitedly told others what He did for them. They shared their testimony.

The devil would like to keep all of us from sharing the gospel. He doesn't want anyone to be saved. He will use every evil, wicked trick he can to keep us from sharing the Good News. He will throw obstacles in our way and distractions around us, to keep us from sharing the Lord with others. He is the enemy of the gospel.

Most believers want to make a difference in this world. If they thought they could, I believe they would. It is the lies of the enemy that hold most people back from doing so. The enemy tells them they can't make a difference and that it really doesn't matter.

You can make a difference. You CAN! The enemy is the one who tells you can't, because he doesn't want anyone to come to the cross and be saved. He wants to take as many people out as he can. He comes to steal, kill, and destroy. He is not only a liar, he is the father of lies.

We must remember satan was defeated at the cross. We have authority over him in our lives. However, he tries to keep us from our Destiny, from being who G-d has called us to be, and to what He has called us. G-d called us to share the gospel of Christ.

The devil wants us to think we aren't qualified. He wants us to think our walk with the Lord isn't perfect enough yet or we haven't gotten to the place in our lives where we are worthy to share the gospel. They are all lies from the pit of hell. Don't believe them.

> *"You are of G-d, little children, and have overcome them, because He Who is in you is greater than he who is in the world."*
>
> ### *I John 4:4 NKJV*

There was a man who lived in the tombs near Gadarenes. He was possessed by many demons. When he met Jesus, the Lord cast the demons out of him. The man was delivered and set free. After his encounter with Jesus, the townspeople found the man clothed in his right mind, sitting peacefully at the feet of the Master. His life was changed completely, *radically*. There was an affect, a transformation. A powerful, miraculous upheaval happened in his life.

The man asked the Lord if he could go with Him, but Jesus told him to go tell his family what G-d did for him. The Bible says that the man did as Jesus told him. He went back to town and testified of G-d's miraculous power and freedom! (Luke 8:26-39)

He gave his testimony of what G-d had done: how the Lord changed His life forever!

We can do the same, as we begin to share the Good News of the gospel with others, by simply sharing our testimony of what G-d did for us in our own lives.

> *"And they overcame him by the blood of the Lamb and by the word of their testimony, and they did not love their lives to the death."*
>
> **Revelation 12:11 NKJV**

Sharing your personal testimony is a good way to begin sharing about Jesus. However, it is good to have training in soul winning. I went through several different evangelism trainings, which were beneficial. Being in a soul-winning training class gives you the opportunity to observe others who are more experienced in soul winning, as well as the opportunity to participate at different levels of involvement. It gives you prayer support and encouragement. I highly recommend that you get into a good soul-winning class.

Final Thoughts

W E, AS BELIEVERS in Jesus Christ, have the answer to the problems people around us face, the sickness they are plagued with, the fear and anxiety they suffer from, and the mental and financial burdens they are dealing with. The answer is Jesus.

If you have received Jesus as your Savior and Lord, you have all you need to share the gospel. His Holy Spirit lives in you and, by His power, He will enable and equip you to share the Good News to make an impact on the world for the Kingdom of G-d.

The same *dynamis* power I spoke of earlier *is in you.* You have access to it through the Holy Spirit who lives in you, as a believer in Jesus Christ.

> *"The Spirit of G-d, Who raised Jesus from the dead, lives in you."*
>
> **Romans 8:11a NLT**

Ask G-d for a passion for souls and the Father's heart of compassion for the lost: a furious, fiery faith *in action*!

Love G-d, above all else, and ask Him for a heart of repentance and obedience toward the Lord.

Ask Him for faith and trust to believe He is who He says He is and that He will do what He says He will do.

Ask for Holy Spirit to fill you to overflowing and to anoint you for His purpose.

Ask the Lord for divine appointments, open doors, and opportunities to share the gospel with others.

Ask for wisdom and discernment as you share the Good News of Jesus Christ.

Lastly, ask Him to have His will and way in your life as you submit yourself to Him and His Kingdom's purpose.

Time is running out! We can't wait any longer. We can't depend on others to share the Good News with the lost around us.

Dear ones, we are the messengers, the ones sent to tell them!

WHAT ABOUT YOU?

P ERHAPS WHILE READING this book, you realized you
never truly received Jesus as your Lord and Savior
and would like to do that today. Or maybe you did
so some time ago but would like to re-dedicate your life
and renew that commitment to the Lord now.

If you would like to do that, please pray this prayer *out
loud, from your heart,* not just your mind or your intellect.

Dear Heavenly Father—

Forgive me of all the wrong things I have done. Wash
and cleanse me. Make me whole and set me free. I receive
Your forgiveness and Your gift of salvation and eternal life.

Jesus, I believe you are the Son of G-d. I believe You
died on the cross for me, rose again, and are sitting at
the right hand of the Father in Heaven. I believe You are
coming back for me someday.

Fill me with Your Holy Spirit. Thank You that You
have made me a new creation, and that I no longer live
in condemnation, guilt, or shame. Give me a deeper
revelation of Your love and the Destiny You have for me.
Thank You for the wonderful plan You have for my life.

Give me a hunger and thirst for You and Your Word.

Give me a passion for You and compassion for the lost. Anoint me and fill me with Your *dynamis* power as I share the gospel with those around me.

Thank You, Lord!

In Jesus' Name,

Amen.

You are a part of G-d's family and the Kingdom of G-d. Share with others what G-d did for you today!

> *"But as many as received Him, to them He gave the right to become children of G-d, to those who believe in His Name."*
>
> **John 1:12 NKJV**

> *"For G-d so loved the world that He gave His only begotten Son, that whoever believes in Him should not perish but have everlasting life."*
>
> **John 3:16 NKJV**

> *"For 'whoever calls on the name of the LORD shall be saved!"*
>
> **Romans 10:13 NKJV**

Congratulations and G-d bless you, dear one!

If you don't have a church home, please find one! We all should get plugged into a Bible-believing, gospel-preaching, Holy Spirit-filled church.

For more information, assistance, resources, and training in soul-winning and personal evangelism contact:

mjvministries.com
MJV Ministries
P.O. Box 8642
Delray Beach, FL 33482

DEEPER WATER

PERHAPS, AS YOU were reading through this book, Holy Spirit brought names of people to mind and spoke into your spirit to share your testimony with them. Perhaps, He has been gently pressing on your heart to share the Good News.

I encourage you by faith, to write those names on the lines below. Please, pray over each one. Ask the Lord to prepare each heart. Ask G-d for ideas and opportunities to share the gospel with them. Listen to what He says.

Then, take a step of faith in obedience and in G-d's love: toss your net into the deeper water and see what G-d does!

_____

_____

_____

_____

_____

_____

_____

Works Cited

Vidulich, Michael J. *Revival in Me.* MJV Ministries, 2022, page 16.

Books by Jeannette Luby

Available on Amazon.com

The Victorious Life Series—

The Victorious Life
Walking in Freedom

Walking Free
A 40-Day Devotional

Other books

G-d's Redeeming Love
A Remarkable Rescue from Darkness

My Beloved
A Love Letter

For children—

Psalm 23
My Safe Place

You can contact Jeannette Luby via email—
thevictoriouslife4ever@gmail.com
Find me on Facebook:
Jeannette Luby

Made in the USA
Columbia, SC
29 March 2024

33777452R00033